Jarrold Moths Se

With text by **Ge**

British Moths
Book 2

Jarrold Colour Publications, Norwich

Although butterflies are widely popular, moths are apt to be regarded with suspicion. The reason for this prejudice is hardly logical, and probably due to moths being associated with other creatures of the night and also witches on account of their nocturnal habits. Today a growing number of people are realising that moths are as interesting as butterflies, and in many instances rival them in beauty. Of our own modest butterfly population only two species are classed as pests because their caterpillars eat cabbages and some other cultivated plants. A number of moths are also unpopular owing to the caterpillars attacking garden plants, but the bulk of them live on weeds or the foliage of common trees and do little harm. Some of the few destructive species belong to the section called Micros because of their modest size, and they include the dreaded clothes moths which although so small can leave a trail of damage in the wardrobe. Then there is the notorious codlin moth, scourge of the orchard, which lives as a caterpillar inside apples and pears. The mill moth, or 'Mediterranean flour moth', introduced into Britain about 1887, has proved to be an undesirable alien, and is now a pest in some flour-mills. Its caterpillars, of grub-like appearance, feed on cereals and other vegetable products as well as flour and meal. A few other harmful moths certainly exist, but fortunately the number is small in proportion to the harmless species.

This book deals with a further selection of interesting, and in most cases, colourful moths, and includes a short section on Micros. Several of the large family Noctuidae were described in Book 1, and a few are also dealt with here, including the large and striking red underwing moth, one of several belonging to the genus *Catocala* found in this country. Its relation the even more imposing blue underwing, or Clifden Nonpareil, long regarded as a rare prize caused a stir among moth-collectors when it was found to be breeding in a wooded part of east Kent. Several more alien species have also become established in the last few years, though in one or two instances their hold is precarious. Moths are greatly influenced by climatic changes and a species may increase or decrease for no other apparent reason. Although they have been studied and collected exhaustively for many years there is still much that we do not know about their economy, and the subject offers endless scope for investigation to young entomologists as well as those of more advanced years.

The subject of 'assembling' is mentioned briefly in Book 1, and the present work also refers to species, including the oak eggar and the fox moth, which are often used in the experiment. The explanation of the term is that male moths of the species spend their short lives searching for the females, and in their efforts often travel considerable distances. They are guided by the scent of the females, and detect this by means of their elaborate antennae fashioned like small feathers, or plumes – the females have simple, hair-like antennae. Moth-hunters take advantage of this attraction by rearing the moths at home, and when a female emerges taking her to a locality where the species is normally found. If conditions are favourable the wild males will pick up the subtle invitation of the female, which should be enclosed in a small cage. The lovelorn suitors will disregard human beings, and become so tame that they can easily be handled. Even if the female is removed from the cage they will continue to flutter around because of the scent it retains. It has been suggested that a kind of wireless message, and not scent, is the explanation of the sexual attraction of these moths, but there are no grounds for treating the idea seriously. Although the favourites for 'assembling' are the day-flying species, the experiment can be extended to some night-fliers such as the puss moth and various hawk moths. When pairing has taken place the unsuccessful males soon lose interest and fly away.

Some examples of the large family called Geometridae are included in this book, which in addition to such attractive species as the numerous thorn moths and their allies includes a number of species found only in autumn and winter. The caterpillars of the family have fewer pro-legs than the usual five pairs, including the anal claspers, of other caterpillars, and they arch the body into a loop when walking. That is why they are called 'loopers' or geometers, and in America 'measuring worms'. Many 'looper' caterpillars are also similar to twigs or stems, and this is useful in protecting them from the sharp eyes of insect-eating birds and other enemies. The caterpillars of a number of species pass the entire winter fully exposed to the weather, and their sole protection is similarity to twigs. In addition to the true winter moth, mentioned more fully in the general text, other geometer moths that appear in autumn and winter include the mottled umber, orange umber, early moth, and spring usher. The males of these differ considerably, but the females though not alike in detail share the common feature of being wingless. This might seem a serious handicap, but it has advantages as it means that the moths concerned are easily overlooked as they rest by day in crevices of bark or inside cracks in fences, etc. After sunset they become more lively and are sought by the males, and when paired they make their way to the twigs to lay their eggs. This can entail a long journey on foot, including climbing the trunks of tall trees, and some are trapped in woods and orchards by the sticky bands placed round the trunks by foresters and gardeners. In spite of this hazard and others, however, many survive, and the caterpillars are usually all too common in the spring. In some years such trees as oak and birch are completely denuded of foliage by early summer, and produce a second crop of leaves later in the season. It is significant that the scientific name of the mottled umber moth is *defoliaria*. Another member of the family is the often discussed peppered moth frequently described as presenting an example of evolutionary changes in our own time. The explanation is that within the last century melanic forms of the moth have replaced the original paler forms in areas affected by industrial smoke. In this respect also it should be noted that melanism has increased considerably in recent years in a number of moths of this family and some other families.

Some other moths described in this book originate from less conventional caterpillars which exist on a diet of wood instead of foliage. They are the goat moth and the leopard moth, of which the latter is classed as a pest by gardeners because its caterpillars sometimes feed inside the trunk or branches of lilac and some other ornamental trees. The caterpillars of the swift moths differ in habits from the majority of caterpillars by living underground, and feeding on roots. They are pale in colour and when unearthed by gardeners are apt to be mistaken for the larvae of ground beetles. The ghost swift, the largest of five species of swift moths, is described and illustrated. Also among internal feeders are the caterpillars of the clearwing moths, which are represented in Britain by several species, but mainly overlooked or mistaken for other types of insects. The caterpillars live in a variety of plants and trees, and locating them calls for both patience and knowledge of their habits. One more likely to be noticed is the caterpillar of the currant clearwing which lives in the stems and twigs of currant bushes, weakening these by eating the pith. It is disliked by fruit-growers, but seems less common and widespread than formerly, perhaps because many of the older, neglected currant bushes in cottage gardens where it was established have been cleared away. The larger hornet clearwings, two species, have a superficial likeness to a true hornet, but of course cannot sting – no moths sting. They are sometimes seen on the trunks of poplars and willows in June and July, and the caterpillars tunnel the wood of these trees.

The Micro moths, as stated, form a vast selection including many genera and hundreds of species, but although the title signifies their limited size some are actually larger than many species of geometers, and have a wing-span in the region of 30 mm. The family Pyralidae includes over 200 species found in Britain, and some are brightly coloured. The numerous grass moths, found commonly in pastures and meadows, belong to the subfamily Crambinae. The moths emerge in summer, and although they rest by day on grasses they are easily disturbed by people walking through the grass. A closer look at one reveals the narrow fore-wings and broader hind-wings, and some are attractively marked with white against a gold-brown background. The even larger family of Micros called Tortricidae includes about 300 British species mainly of small size, but with broader fore-wings than moths of the previous family. When at rest with folded wings they look bell-shaped, and many tortrix moths, as they are known, have rather dull colours. An exception and better-known member of the family is the green tortrix (*Tortrix viridana*) which is found in oak woods. Its wriggling caterpillars are very destructive to oak leaves, and are classed as serious pests by foresters. They are usually hidden from view in rolled-up leaves. The moth has bright green fore-wings. The largest of all the families of Micro moths is called Tinaeoidea and includes the smallest of all British moths, of which some have a wing-span of only 3 mm. Although so modest in size, however, some of these minute moths are very brightly marked and their wings reflect vivid metallic colours. The already mentioned clothes moths are also in the family. The plume moths, so called because their narrow wings are divided into sections fashioned like small feathers, are neglected by many lepidopterists. They certainly deserve more attention. One of the better-known species is described and figured.

This book contains descriptions and pictures from photographs of moths of different families. They include some noctuids, the oak eggar and a few of its handsome relations, and the gaudy tiger moths. Several of the many geometers are also included, and the strange goat moth. Reference to the many Micros can only be brief in so limited a work. The majority of the pictures are in colour, and in some instances, for unavoidable reasons, are larger than life, but in every case the wing-span, or other relevant measurements, are shown at the end of the single-line captions. Following modern practice all measurements are given in millimetres.

Book 1 of this series on British moths contains references to some of the numerous Noctuidae family, and several more species are included here. The Red Underwing is larger than many of the other species, and also very brightly coloured on the hind-wings. It comes out in late summer, and is commonest in the south and south-east of England, but also found as far north as Yorkshire. The long, greyish caterpillar feeds on both poplar and willow, and is hard to recognise when resting on a twig. The pupa is enclosed in a tough silken cocoon, and has a coating of bluish powder.

A number of moths called Plusias have conspicuous metallic markings, the commonest being the Silver-Y which flies both by day and night. It has been found in most of Britain at one time or another, but is migratory and fluctuates in numbers from year to year. It was scarce in 1972 but very common in 1973. The green caterpillar feeds on nettle and other weeds, and the blackish pupa is inside a whitish cocoon.

The Figure of Eight moth takes its name from the markings on the fore-wings, but these vary with more perfect 'eights' in some specimens than others. Its distribution includes much of England, especially in wooded areas. The fleshy, yellow and blue caterpillar has contrasting black dots.

1

2

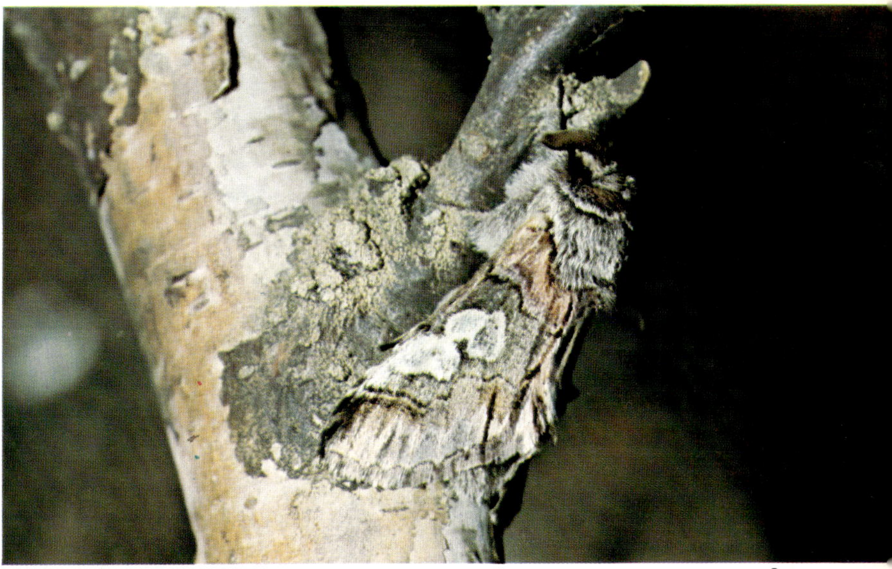

3

1. **RED UNDERWING** *(Catocala nupta)* Male 78 mm.

2. **SILVER-Y** *(Plusia gamma)* Male 38 mm.

3. **FIGURE OF EIGHT** *(Episema caeruleocephala)* Male 36 mm.

4

5

4. **LACKEY** *(Malacosoma neustria)* Caterpillars 45 mm. long.

5. **HERALD** *(Scoliopteryx libatrix)* Male 46 mm.

6. **OAK EGGAR** *(Lasiocampa quercus)* Female and Cocoon 76 mm. long.

The Herald moth was called the 'Furbelow' by some early entomologists, and its colours are very attractive. It appears in late summer and hibernates during the winter. Its range covers a large part of Britain, and its slender green caterpillar feeds on both willow and poplar. It is soon alarmed and falls to the ground if disturbed.

The small brown or buff-yellow Lackey moth belongs to the family Lasiocampidae, which includes several more interesting species. Its caterpillars are more striking in appearance, however. They are gregarious and share a common web, or tent, of whitish silk. Their foodplants include hawthorn, blackthorn, and rose, which makes them unpopular in gardens. The moth flies in July and August.

Other moths of this family include the Oak Eggar, so named because its cocoon is shaped like an acorn even though it does not live on oak trees. The female is larger and paler in colour than the red-brown male, and the large hairy caterpillar feeds on bramble, heather, hawthorn, and other plants. It hibernates in winter and completes its growth in the spring. The moths emerge in July and the males fly by day, spending their short life in search of the females. A virgin female reared at home will usually attract a number of males. The very similar Northern Eggar, a subspecies, replaces the Oak Eggar in northern England, Scotland and parts of Wales.

6

7. **FOX** *(Macrothylacia rubi)* Male 50 mm.

8. **DRINKER** *(Philudoria potatoria)* Female 62 mm.

9. **DRINKER** *(Philodoria potatoria)* Caterpillar 60 mm. long.

7

8

9

The Fox moth owes its name to the caterpillar which has a thick coat of tawny and black hairs. It feeds on heather and other moorland plants, also birch, and can be found in late summer and early autumn before it goes into hibernation. On waking in the spring it does not feed, but eventually spins a cocoon and changes into a pupa. The moth emerges in June, and the males fly in early evening searching for the female. An unpaired female will attract males. On one occasion on a Yorkshire moor the author 'assembled' over forty males. After pairing the female lays batches of oval, brown eggs on heather and other plants. The species is common in much of Britain.

The Drinker moth is so called because its hairy caterpillar, which feeds on grass and reeds, is said to have a liking for dew, but this is probably an exaggeration. When fully fed it spins a long, narrow cocoon of brownish silk in which to pupate. The moths appear in July and August, and the males, usually of rich red-brown colour, are smaller than the females. They fly by night and sometimes enter lighted rooms. The species is well distributed and common in some areas, but has become scarcer in recent years in others, perhaps because of the drastic trimming of road verges.

10

The imposing Lappet moth is the largest member of the family Lasiocampidae, but the male is smaller than the female. Both sexes rest by day, but the male is very active after dark and sometimes attracted by house-lights. The strange name of the species is due to the fleshy projections, or lappets, from the body of the caterpillar which feeds on hawthorn, blackthorn, and various orchard trees. It grows to 100 mm. long. The species is commonest in south and south-east England, but its range extends to Yorkshire.

The footmen moths of the family Lithosiinae owe their name to a fanciful likeness to a standing footman as they rest with closed wings. There are some fifteen species, and the Common Footman is the most distributed. Its range covers most of England and parts of Scotland. It flies in July, and the dark grey, bristly caterpillar feeds on lichens. The caterpillars of the other footmen moths are also mainly lichen feeders, and as lichen is adversely affected by impure air the moths are commoner in clean rural areas.

The Buff Ermine moth belongs to the family Arctiidae which also includes the tiger moths. It is common in much of Britain, and its markings vary considerably. Some examples have heavy black lines. The hairy caterpillar is a smaller type of 'Woolly Bear', and feeds on such weeds as nettle and dandelion.

10. **LAPPET** *(Gastropacha quercifolia)* Male 62 mm.

11. **COMMON FOOTMAN** *(Lithosia lurideola)* Male 35 mm.

12. **BUFF ERMINE** *(Spilosoma lubricepida)* Male 38 mm.

11

12

The Garden Tiger moth and its caterpillar are known by many who do not usually take an interest in moths. Its brilliant, contrasting colours are a good example of 'warning colours', but subject to considerable variation. Some remarkable varieties occur among wild stock, and others are produced in captivity. They include specimens with unspotted yellow hind-wings and pale cream fore-wings, also others with entirely blue hind-wings and chocolate-coloured fore-wings. The caterpillar, the true 'Woolly Bear', has a thick coat of hair. It hibernates during the winter, and becomes fully grown in spring. Its foodplants include such weeds as dock and dandelion, but not many cultivated plants. In captivity, under the influence of extra warmth, it can sometimes be induced to continue feeding in the autumn, and moths may be produced in the winter months.

The Cream-spot Tiger, also a handsome moth, with cream markings on its black fore-wings, and orange and black hind-wings, is a more local species found mainly in south and south-east England.

The Cinnabar is another exotic-looking moth with vermilion or deep pink hind-wings. It flies in May and is common in much of Britain. Examples with yellow hind-wings are found occasionally, and a rare race originating in Dorset has all the wings bright red.

13

14

15

13. **GARDEN TIGER** *(Arctia caja)* Male 60 mm.

14. **CINNABAR** *(Callimorpha jacobaeae)* Male 38 mm.

15. **GARDEN TIGER** *(Arctia caja)* Caterpillar 45 mm. long.

16. CINNABAR *(Callimorpha jacobaeae)* Caterpillars 32 mm. long.

17. ORANGE UNDERWING *(Archieris parthenias)* Male 35 mm.

18. JERSEY TIGER *(Euplagia quadripunctaria)* Female 56 mm.

16

17

39

The Small Ermine moth (*Yponomeuta cognatella*) is one of several rather similar species to be seen during the summer, and it is often very common. Its narrow fore-wings marked with black dots give a streamlined appearance as it rests on a leaf, and it soon takes flight if disturbed.

Three caterpillars of the Honey moth are shown in the picture. The moth has narrow buff-coloured fore-wings, and paler hind-wings, but is small in size. It can be seen from June until early autumn, usually in the vicinity of beehives. The caterpillars feed on beeswax, and seem to prefer older samples. They can be very destructive in hives, and if disturbed they often perform strange contortions. The species has been found in much of England and Wales, and is classed as a pest by bee-keepers.

The dainty plume moths belong to the family Pterophoridae, and some twenty-three species are found in Britain. But several closely resemble each other and it requires expert knowledge to identify them. One of the best known and easy to recognise is the White Plume moth which appears in June and July, and can be seen resting on plants and fences. It takes wing if alarmed, but does not usually fly far. Its caterpillar lives on bindweed and hibernates during the winter. The species is common in much of England and Wales.

40. SMALL ERMINE *(Yponomeuta cognatella)* Caterpillars 10 mm. long.

40

The Small Ermine moth is mentioned on the previous page, and the gregarious caterpillars, which share a common web, or tent, are shown here. They shelter in this, and feed voraciously on spindle leaves, often denuding a large branch of foliage. If disturbed they wriggle violently, and when fully grown they spin small silken cocoons. The species should not be confused with the rather larger Thistle Ermine (*Myelois cribrumella*) which belongs to a different family, and lives as a caterpillar on thistles.

18

The caterpillars of the Cinnabar moth are marked with alternate rings of black and orange-yellow. A good case of 'warning colours'. They feed on ragwort during the summer, and because they are gregarious soon strip the plants. Ragwort is a troublesome weed, and unfortunately it has been introduced into some other countries, so to check its further spread caterpillars of the cinnabar have been sent to the affected places.

The Jersey Tiger is one of the most colourful of all moths, but because of its restricted distribution in Britain few people ever see it alive. Its limited haunts are in south Devon, and it appears in July and August. Although normally a night-flier, it takes wing if disturbed in the daytime. A handsome variety has the red of the hind-wings replaced by yellow. The orange, cream, and black caterpillar feeds on dead nettle, dandelion, and other weeds.

The Orange Underwing moth belongs to the family Archiearinae, and is a day-flying species. It appears in late March and April, and is found in birch woods in much of England, but less widely in Scotland. The caterpillar feeds on birch leaves and catkins. The moths are mainly active in sunny weather and visit sallow catkins. The Pale Orange Underwing, a similar-looking moth, but with slightly different antennae, is found among aspens in woods as far north as Huntingdon.

19

Another large assortment of moths belong to the family Geometridae, which includes several subfamilies and many attractive species. The moths have slender bodies, and some rest with the wings pressed together over the back like butterflies. The caterpillars, as mentioned before, are called 'loopers'. The Blotched Emerald is one of several green moths called 'emeralds'. It flies in June and July, and is locally distributed in wooded areas mainly in southern England. The caterpillar feeds on oak, and is noted for adorning itself with fragments of leaf and bud-scales which help to protect it from enemies.

The Yellow Shell is found almost throughout Britain, and often advertises its presence in the daytime by fluttering out of a hedge or bush, flying a few yards and alighting again. It has a range of colour variation, and some specimens are barred with deep brown. A dwarf form is found in the Hebrides and other Scottish islands. The caterpillar feeds on a number of different weeds and also grass.

The Argent and Sable moth is striking in appearance, and makes little attempt to hide. It often flies by day, and is found in many places in Britain where birch trees are common. A smaller, heavily marked race occurs in Sutherlandshire and some other parts of Scotland. The blackish caterpillar feeds on birch and hides between leaves fastened together by silk.

19. BLOTCHED EMERALD *(Comibaena pustulata)* Female 30 mm.

20. YELLOW SHELL *(Euphyia bilineata)* Female 29 mm.

21. ARGENT AND SABLE *(Rheumaptera hastata)* Female 30 mm.

20

21

The Magpie or Currant moth needs little introduction for it is often seen in gardens. It comes out in July and is well established in much of Britain. Its markings are subject to considerable variation, and by selective breeding in captivity many remarkable forms have been produced including the almost black variety Varleyata. The creamy white, black-dotted caterpillar is shown on the next page.

A few moths of this large family appear in late autumn, and include the Winter moth, which although modest in appearance is significant in the economic sense. The male has grey-brown wings and can be seen fluttering at dusk, but the wingless female is noticed less often as she rests on bark. After pairing she lays her eggs on a wide range of trees and shrubs, and the caterpillars on hatching in the spring are very destructive.

The fifty or so small moths known as 'pugs' are worth studying, and one of the most attractive species is the Netted Pug which has a net-like pattern on the fore-wings. It is common in many parts of Britain, and flies in June. Its rather stumpy caterpillar feeds on the unripe seeds of bladder campion and sea campion. As some pug moths are very similar to each other in markings it is advisable, when possible, to rear them from caterpillars.

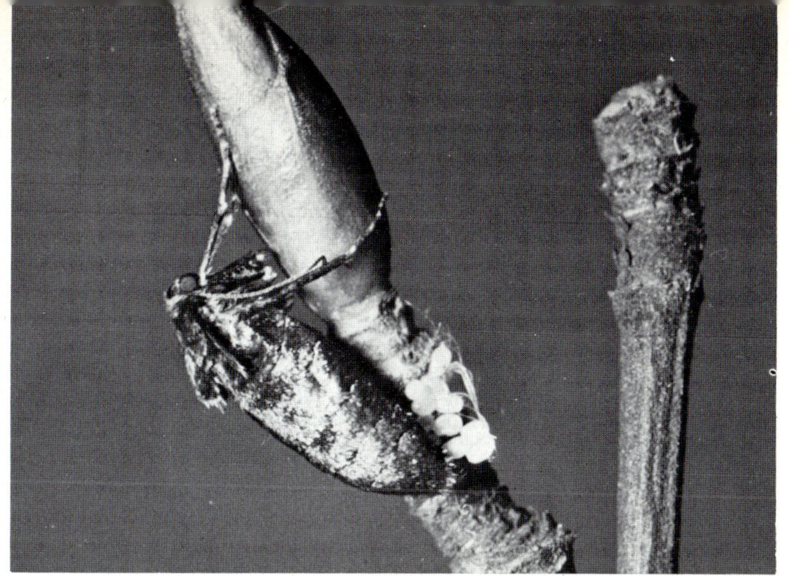

23

24

22. **MAGPIE OR CURRANT** *(Abraxas grossulariata)* Male 50 mm.

23. **WINTER** *(Operophtera brumata)* Female laying eggs 6 mm. long.

24. **NETTED PUG** *(Eupithecia venosta)* Female 20 mm.

25. MAGPIE OR CURRANT *(Abraxas grossulariata)* Caterpillar 32 mm. long.

26. SWALLOWTAIL *(Ourapteryx sambucaria)* Male 56 mm.

27. LUNAR THORN *(Selenia lunaria)* Male 40 mm.

25

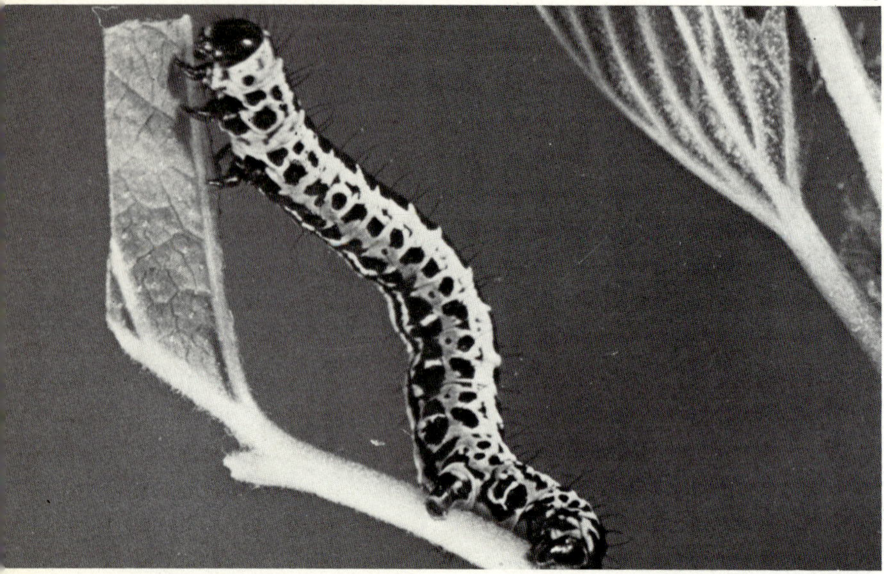

26

27

The looping caterpillars of the Magpie moth are as well known as their parent, but the two are not always associated by gardeners. In addition to feeding on currant they eat euonymus, gooseberry, and blackthorn. They hibernate low down on the foodplant during the winter, and complete their growth in the spring. Although conspicuous they are usually avoided by birds. The shiny black pupa has yellow rings.

The graceful Swallowtail moth comes out in July, and is common in many parts of England. It is frequently seen in gardens flying on its ample wings in the early evening. Its slender caterpillar feeds on both hawthorn and blackthorn, but seems to prefer a diet of ivy. It hibernates in winter and finally changes into a pupa inside a silken hammock among the leaves.

Several attractive moths are called 'thorns' because the caterpillars of some are remindful of thorny twigs. The Lunar Thorn is not one of the commonest, but is among the more handsome species. It comes out in late May and June, and although local is found in much of Britain as far north as the Orkneys. The caterpillar feeds in late summer and can be seen on different woodland trees including oak, birch, and blackthorn. The Early Thorn, a well-known species that appears in late March and April is double-brooded, and the second generation appears in July.

28

29

28. PEPPERED *(Biston carbonaria)* Female melanic form 60 mm.

29. PEPPERED *(Biston carbonaria)* Caterpillar 50 mm. long.

30. GOAT *(Cossus cossus)* Female 85 mm.

The Peppered moth has been given special attention because of its variation in colour according to locality, and this has also led to numerous experiments. Type examples of the moth are white dotted, or 'peppered', with black, and thus very different from moths of the melanic form in which all the wings are mainly black. The former are found chiefly in clean rural areas, and the darker ones inhabit places where there is less atmospheric dirt. It means, therefore, that the moths have protective markings wherever they exist. A pale example resting on a clean tree-trunk tends to match this, while a melanic specimen on a blackened tree is also camouflaged, and its natural enemies are deceived. The slender caterpillar feeds on numerous different trees in both woodland and garden, including oak, lime and rose. The species is well distributed in much of Britain, and in some places intermediate examples with a proportion of both light and dark markings are found. Similar freak forms are also reared in captivity.

The Goat Moth is larger than most of our moths, but lacks bright colours. It belongs to the family Cossidae, and the English name really applies to the caterpillar, shown overleaf, which has a scent like that of a he-goat. The female moth is larger than the male, but in spite of her bulk her sombre shades are protective as she rests on a tree-trunk.

30

31

The caterpillar of the Goat moth has been mentioned on the previous page. It is also unconventional in habit as it ignores the foliage of plants and trees and exists on a diet of wood, especially that of elm, poplar, and willow. It feeds for as long as three years, but when fully grown leaves the tree to wander off before spinning a large cocoon in which to spend the winter. Pupation takes place in the following spring and the moth emerges in July. The species is found in much of Britain, but is often overlooked.

The Leopard moth belongs to the same family as the Goat moth, but is very different in appearance. The early stages of the two are similar, however, as the pale caterpillar of the present species also eats wood. It can be a pest when it attacks lilacs and other garden trees, but it also affects ash trees. The moth appears in July and is fairly common in parts of southern England, and found at least as far north as Yorkshire.

The highly coloured, day-flying burnet moths belong to the family Zygaenidae, and the Five-spot Burnet is one of the commonest. It is well distributed, though local, in southern England, and its range extends to the midlands. It appears in late May and June, and its caterpillar feeds on bird's-foot trefoil and some other vetches.

31. GOAT *(Cossus cossus)* Caterpillar 80 mm. long.

32. FIVE-SPOT BURNET *(Zygaena trifolii)* Male. 32 mm.

33. LEOPARD *(Zeuzera pyrinia)* Female 60 mm.

32

33

The Ghost Swift moth of the family Hepialidae is one of five different swift moths found in Britain. It is common in many areas, and the male has a strange swaying flight which can be seen at dusk in late June and July. Because his wings are white on the upper surface and dusky underneath he seems to appear and then quickly disappear alternately. The female has yellowish-brown wings marked with orange. The root-feeding caterpillars affect many different weeds and some garden plants.

Mimicry is widespread in insects, and some examples exist in the moths called 'clearwings'. They belong to the family Sesiidae, and resemble flies, hornets, etc. The Six-belted Clearwing has yellow belts, seven in the male and six in the female and can be mistaken for a small wasp. It appears in July and is found mainly in south and south-west England. Its caterpillar feeds on the roots of bird's-foot trefoil.

As mentioned in the Introduction, a large number of moths are termed Micros because of limited size, but they vary considerably in this respect. The Mother of Pearl moth, of the family Pyralidae, is an example of a larger species, and it can be seen during July among nettles in much of Britain and Ireland. Its lively caterpillar lives on nettles and fastens leaves together with silk.

34

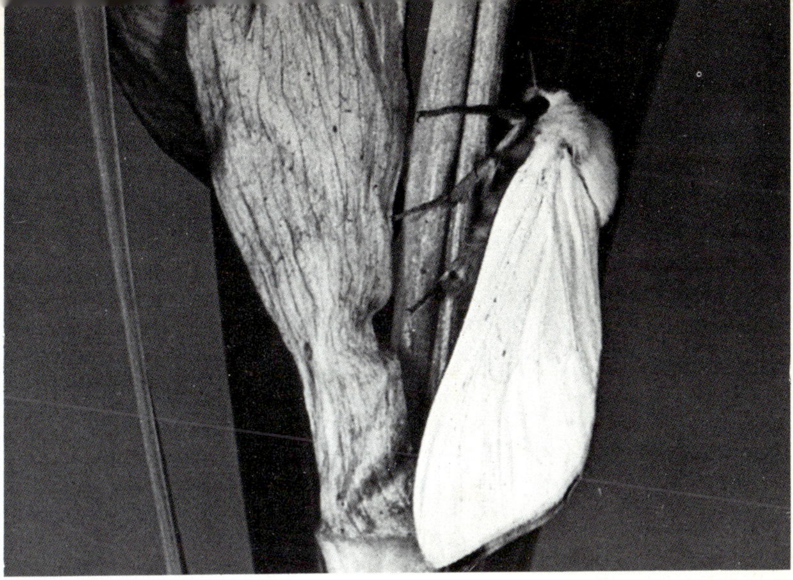

35

36

34. **MOTHER OF PEARL** *(Sylepta ruralis)* Male 34 mm.

35. **GHOST SWIFT** *(Hepialus humili)* Male 50 mm.

36. **SIX-BELTED CLEARWING** *(Dipsosphecia scopigra)* Male 22 mm.

37. SMALL ERMINE *(Yponomeuta cognatella)* Male 20 mm.

38. HONEY *(Achroia grisella)* Caterpillars 15 mm. long.

39. WHITE PLUME *(Alucita pentadactyla)* Male 30 mm.

37

38

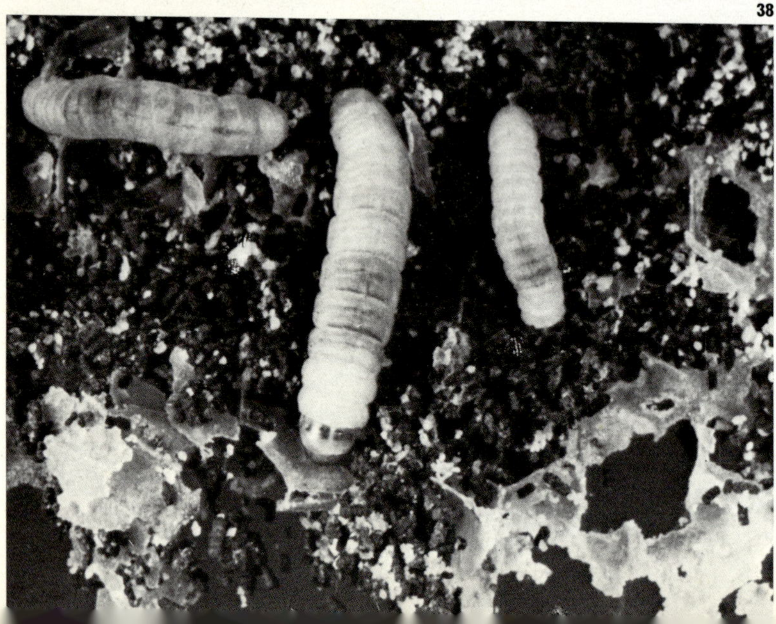